awkward to awesome

First Edition

Printed in the United States

ISBN-13: 978-1-9163004-0-8
ISBN-10: 1-9163004-0-5

TABLE OF CONTENTS

Introduction ix

Chapter One: Confidence 1

Quiz Time 15

Chapter Two: Family 21

Interview with Super Sienna 31

Chapter Three: Puberty 41

Chapter Four: Squad 51

Chapter Five: Your Personal Space 59

Chapter Six: Travelling 67

Time Warp 77

Chapter Seven: Money 95

Chapter Eight: Fashion, Beauty and Hair 103

Chapter Nine: Going Out by Yourself 131

Chapter Ten: Food 137

Chapter Eleven: Happiness 153

Ask Mia 165

Chapter Twelve: Messing Up 173

Your Time to Shine 181

Acknowledgements 215

Introduction

HI MIACORNS!

My name's Mia, and I'm a YouTuber. I'm also a big sister, I'm vegan, I love fashion, and sometimes I'm a super-awkward teen!

I know that lots of you relate, so I've created this book on my top tips for going from Awkward to Awesome! In this book, I'm going to cover loads of different topics that you guys always ask me about, from periods to dealing with losing friends.

Of course, I'm no expert and nobody's perfect, but I want everybody to feel like they can shine and be authentically themselves, and I hope that by writing this book, I will help at least one person in their ambition to be their best self.

But before we get onto the book, here are a few facts about moi:

♡ I **love** eating cereal dry! I hate it when it gets all soggy, because it feels like a waste! My favourite thing is to have a bowlful of dry cereal and eat it like popcorn.

♡ So far I have been to sixteen countries (England, Sri Lanka, Ireland, Germany, the Canary Islands, Spain, Norway, Denmark, Italy, Portugal, the UAE, China, Indonesia, Georgia, Oman and the USA), but there are so many more I'd like to travel to.

♡ I absolutely love etymology. TBH, anything language related interests me so much. I just love how all languages connect in some way and there's always a historical reason to it. I can currently speak English and intermediate Spanish, but my goal is to be able to speak at least four languages fluently.

♡ My thumbs are different shapes! It's a genetic thing where basically one of my bones is shorter than the other. The scientific name for it is *brachydactyly type D*, but there are a lot of nicknames: stub thumb, murderer's thumb, club thumb, bohemian thumb and potter's thumb! It doesn't really bother me because nobody notices it, but I can't use stick-on nails because they never fit my thumb!

♡ I love drawing, so much so that all the pictures in this book were actually drawn by me! Anything arts and crafts is my fave. In fact, I even went through a knitting phase when I was eleven. I'd spend hours knitting these little coats for rescue chickens.

♡ I really like learning about stupid and pointless things. Did you know that strawberries aren't actually berries, but bananas are? Did you know in the painting of Mona Lisa, she doesn't have any eyebrows because in the Renaissance times it was popular to shave them off? Did you know that there are more stars in space than grains of sand on earth? I know, crazy!

Anyways, enough about me. Let's get on to YOU!

Confidence

"Wanting to be
someone else is a waste
of the person you are."

I was about to go to my first-ever rock-climbing class, and I was incredibly nervous. On the drive there I was thinking about **EVERYTHING** that could possibly go wrong, even the most ridiculous things. When I arrived I saw a girl who looked about my age sitting in the area where the receptionist told me to go. I had two options: Sit on the furthest table away from her and pretend to look at my phone until the class started (no risk, but also no possibility of making friends) OR go up to her and say, "Are you here for the teen classes?" (risk of her not wanting to talk and getting rejected, but at least there was a chance of her wanting to make friends). All this went through my head in the space of about two seconds, and I made my choice. What do you think I did? I took the risk and we immediately became friends. It turned out that she recognised me from my YouTube videos and was happy that there was another girl at the class since it was mainly boys.

This isn't the only time this scenario has happened to me, and sometimes I do take the easy option. But every time I do, I always regret it. I'd much rather embarrass myself than forever wonder what the outcome could've been. This IS way easier said than done, and it's common to feel like some people are simply born confident and that you weren't. This, however, is NOT true! Everybody feels insecure at times, and it just depends on whether you dare to step outside your comfort zone or stay inside. Don't compare your flaws to someone else's strengths—that's just silly!

Have you ever experienced that feeling where you think your stomach is tying itself into a complicated sailor's knot and you're certain there's some sort of impending doom coming? Me too. It's normal to feel anxious at times, but it's important to learn how to control it and use it to YOUR advantage, rather than letting it control you. Generally, as a rule of thumb, there are two reasons you can be anxious:

1. You're nervous because you are doing something that is outside of your comfort zone. Lots of people feel as if this type of anxiety is a bad feeling and that you have to avoid it at all costs. But I feel like this attitude actually makes it worse

because when you inevitability do feel this way, you then get anxious about being anxious! Believe it or not, as long as it's managed well, this anxiety can be used for good. Instead of freaking out and letting your emotions overcome you, take a step back and realise that this is your body's way of telling you that you're exiting your comfort zone into unknown territory. This same feeling is the one our ancestors felt that kept them from getting eaten, so it's simply a part of our automatic reaction to new situations. However, that doesn't mean we can't choose to react differently. Instead, use this feeling to motivate you as it's a sign that if you continue, you will grow as a person. **Write down three times you felt this type of anxiety and what you could've done to help the situation instead of freaking out:**

1 _____

_____

_____

_____

_____

_____

_____

_____

_____

_____

2 _____

_____

_____

_____

_____

_____

_____

_____

3 _____

_____

_____

_____

_____

_____

_____

2. You're worrying about something that happened in the past or might happen in the future. While the other type of anxiety can be used for good, this type of anxiety is super unproductive. If there's something you're worrying about and you've done everything possible to help the situation, then there's no point worrying. I know it's super difficult because with the first type once you've done the task, you'll actually feel elated. But with this you don't get that satisfaction. Next time you feel like this, **write down your worries on a piece of paper. Then rip it up and put it in the recycling.** I know you may feel a bit silly, but this really helps your mind get over it.

Everybody has felt self-conscious or shy at some point. When I'm in a new situation I sometimes go into myself because I'm nervous about what other people think of me. This can actually backfire though. To the other person it can come across as if you're moody, when in reality you're just feeling awkward. One phrase I always like to remember is as follows:

People aren't thinking about

YOU

They're thinking about

THEMSELVES

Being shy is a choice that, surprisingly, **you** have control over. **You** can choose to be an introverted person or **not**! Luck, your parents or anybody else aren't the ones deciding, just YOU.

♡ Try smiling. Smiling not only helps YOU feel better (scientific fact), but it also makes you seem more open and approachable—even when you don't feel that way at all! It's so simple, and if people do wonder why you're smiling at a brick wall, it's better than them thinking you're not into making friends.

♡ Have an alter ego. When I feel shy I find that I end up overthinking things, which always turns into a spiral of negative thoughts. One way to combat this is to imagine you're a new character. Become the best version of yourself, like when you've started New Year's resolutions and you imagine that you're a "new" you. Every time you feel yourself holding back, ask yourself: "What would the new me do?" and then act upon that. Your alter ego doesn't have to be you though; it could be a celebrity or a completely made-up person! There are also a lot of famous people that use this technique—even the queen of confidence, Beyoncé, who becomes Sasha Fierce on stage.

♡ **Repeated exposure.** Everything is easier the more times you attempt it. If you never face your fears, you'll never overcome them. This can be difficult, I know, but if you force yourself to do the small things, like smiling at a stranger, this can actually make you more confident to do the big things. Here's a challenge: every day for a week do one thing that you'd normally feel self-conscious doing. Start small and work your way up.

You may have noticed me talking about your comfort zone a lot, lol. All the things that feel easy to do, like brushing your teeth or putting on socks are inside your comfort zone. Things that feel difficult, like starting a new school or asking out your crush, are things outside your comfort zone. Everyone has different levels, but every time you do something that seems scary, your comfort zone gets bigger. One thing that has really boosted my confidence is learning Spanish. It's so nerve-wracking to talk to someone in a language that you don't fully understand. What if you sound like an idiot? Or you accidentally say something offensive? You'd be surprised, but people appreciate it when you've put in the effort, even if you **are** really bad.

♡ Learn to do something you've always been too scared to try, like playing an instrument.
♡ Completely change up your style for a day.
♡ Meet up with a friend you haven't spoken to in a while.
♡ Play a dare game with your friends.
♡ Go to the gym.
♡ Start up that YouTube channel you've always wanted. Sharing your thoughts and opinions with the world can feel scary!
♡ Try a new food.

There are two types of people with small egos: the ones who are shy and don't stand up for themselves, and the ones who talk down to others and act as if they're the best. You may be thinking, hang on, Mia, isn't the second one someone WITH a big ego? Well, deep down, they're not as self-assured as you think they are. They're good at masking their insecurities and taking it out on others. The dictionary definition of ego is as follows:

noun

a person's sense of self-esteem or self-importance.

Some people think having a big ego is a bad thing, but I don't think that's true. It's actually a good thing! It doesn't mean that you don't care about others. Instead, it means that you stand up for yourself, you're strong and determined, you know what you want from life and you're confident in your body and with your personality. If you want to reach your full potential, you have to be full of yourself and have high self-esteem. Who only wants to be half as great as they can be? To truly love yourself, you have to believe you're important. You're not better than others, but you're still special because **everybody's** special. So how can you get a big ego? By supporting yourself. Every time you look in the mirror tell yourself a positive affirmation like, "I'm strong, beautiful and confident." Stick with this for a month and see how you feel at the end. You may feel a bit stupid at first, but the more you say it, the more you'll believe it.

Throughout time people's opinions on what is supposedly "perfect" has changed. Trends come and go, so don't get too caught up on changing yourself depending on what's currently hot. One of the best qualities a person can have is originality. I have red hair, freckles, and pale skin. Some people may bully me for this, but I don't let other people's opinions affect me. When I was younger I used to dislike my hair, but now I've realised that it's part of what makes me unique and stand out against the rest of the crowd. Nobody's "normal" and everyone's unique, so we need to start celebrating our differences, as they are what make us, us.

At the end of the day, don't let the small things get to you. There will be times when you feel like you're on top of the world. There also will be times when you just want to crawl under the covers and hide there. Forever. One bad day does not mean that every day will be like that. There's **always** something to be grateful for, and right now you have something in your life that you take for granted but another person would die for. Confidence comes from you loving and accepting yourself, even your flaws—not from how many likes your Instagram pictures get.

Quiz
TIME!
☆

My favourite thing to do in magazines is always the activities, more than reading the actual content! I'm a major fan of quizzes (especially ones to do with your horoscope), so I decided to make a quiz to help you tell whether you're stuck in your comfort zone or not! Just keep track of your answers, and the symbol you get the most will tell you how far out of your comfort zone you normally get.

You'll try something new, even without knowing if you'll succeed:

Totally!

No. Way.

Sometimes . . .

You freak out if you make a mistake:

No, it doesn't bother me.

It depends on what I did.

I hate it!

How do you feel if you compare yourself to others?

It makes me feel bad.

It doesn't really bother me.

I'm motivated by others' success.

You'll keep trying, even after other people have given up:

Always. In fact, it's better because I have less competition and more chance of succeeding!

Occasionally.

Never, better to be safe than sorry! ♡

You most commonly think:

I'm good at a lot of things.

I can't do a lot of things. ♡

I can do some things, but most people are better than me.

Mostly ♡s: Your natural reaction is to stay inside your comfort zone, and you can do that if you want. However, if you feel like this is because you're scared of failure or rejection, you might want to help push yourself past those self-imposed limiting boundaries to reach your full potential! You can do this by starting small and doing something you'd normally avoid, then increasing this over time.

You're getting there. Don't worry if one day you feel like you haven't made any progress or that you've even declined. This is natural. You can help combat this by keeping yourself positive and motivated by doing more and more nerve-wracking things! You can do it!

Well done. You tend to get out of your comfort zone a lot! Remember that even though you can progress, you can also regress if you overdo it. To avoid this, keep on top of your health and how you're doing mentally. But other than that, keep at it!

Family ♡

The greatest moments
in life are not
concerned with selfish
achievements but rather
with the things we do
for the people we love
and esteem.

Family can be amazing, but they can also be incredibly annoying. Unlike friends, you don't get to choose 'em. So here are my ways of dealing with them, and even getting on with them.

Family isn't "perfect", and all families are unique. Even if you're not related by blood, it doesn't mean they don't want the best for you. I understand that it may be difficult to accept a step-parent, but you should always give them a chance. Try spending as much time as possible with them, and really try to get to know them. You may feel like you're completely different, but you'd be surprised, you might have more in common than you expect. I can't remember my parents being together, and I was only five when my mum met Darren (my stepdad), so it's always been like this for me. I recommend that you talk to them and find out what you're both comfortable with. Do you want to call them mum/dad or by their first name? There's no right way to do things, so you just have to work it out for your situation.

You only live once, so treasuring the moment and spending time with family are vital. It's as simple as setting the table and having a meal together. Talk to your family about how you're feeling, and ask them about how they feel. Go for a walk, to the beach, or on a family run! What's funny is that my family and I spend so much time together that sometimes we end up bickering. It's important to have a happy medium: have dedicated family time and dedicated me time so you appreciate both more. (More on this in the personal space chapter, page 53).

I love going to my grandparents' house. It's loads of fun and feels really cosy. It's especially important to spend lots of time with them because they're not always gonna be there. One day I had a realisation that my grandparents were kids during WW2, which seems crazy to me! I was really curious about how life was then, so I decided to ask them. It's so weird because even though people obviously had other things going on in their lives, I can't imagine what it would be like to wake up and know that your country is at war and still live a normal life. Your grandparents have experienced so much, and it's really important to speak to them to know what life was like and learn from their mistakes. Even though they grew up without Wi-Fi, it doesn't mean that there's not something to learn from them. Another benefit is all the treats! Every time I go to my grandparents' house, they always make some yummy food, and they have some crystallised ginger in the kitchen. Me and my sister (Sienna) end up eating so much that we feel sick!

Asking for things can be incredibly difficult, but it can be an amazing skill to learn. Here's my formula on how you would ask your parents/guardians if you're allowed to wear makeup:

1. **Be reasonable and think it through.** Why do you want to start wearing makeup? How often are you going to wear it? Ask yourself these types of questions.

2. **Have points about why they should let you do this.** For example, you might say, "It's an amazing art form and I really want to get creative", and, "I'm going to post my looks on Instagram. It'll be a great project for me to work on".

3. **Be prepared for denial.** There are two ways this could go:

> "I feel like you're trying to grow up too fast."
> "YOU'RE SO UNFAIR!" *stomps upstairs and slams door*
> Or
> "I feel like you're trying to grow up too fast."
> "I understand why you might think this, but I'll only wear it indoors, if you want. This would also be a great project and experience for me, and I could show people my Instagram account in the future as proof of what I can achieve."

In which scenario do you feel like they're more likely to change their mind? The second one, right?

4. **You may have to meet each other in the middle.** The result may be that you're only allowed to wear makeup on the weekends at home. If you prove how responsible you are by being able to have a mature conversation, they may realise that you're more grown up than they originally thought.

Every situation is different, and you may still get an outright no. Try to understand why they might say this and remember that they don't want to be intentionally annoying, they just want the best for you. They know how it feels to ask an adult for things, as they have been a kid before, so try not to have hard feelings.

If you want to be close with your family and have a good relationship with them, you need to be open and honest. Sometimes lying may feel like the easier option, but in the long term they will always find out and it'll be worse than telling the truth. You'd be surprised, if you tell the truth in the first place, they may not end up telling you off. But if you lie, they'll definitely be disappointed in you. Not telling the truth is one of those easy but very bad habits to fall into. It starts with little things, like lying about staying out an extra half an hour with your friends. Instead of making up an excuse, admit that you lost track of time. Your parents may be annoyed that you didn't pay attention, but they will trust you with the bigger and more important things. I've lied to my parents, and not only does it make you feel bad, but also it creates distance between you. Here's a challenge: For the next twenty-four hours, catch yourself every time you go to lie and keep a tally on your phone to see how much you're actually doing it. This can help you realise all the little, and seemingly harmless, white lies you tell. Remember that no lie is a good one. I'm not saying that you should tell your mum that her new dress is horrible when she asks your opinion, but you could say, "I personally don't think that's your best colour. Do they have it in red?" Or "It's okay, but I feel like you could do better".

I have two sisters (plus a brother on the way), and I love them so much, but they can get on my nerves. Sienna (eight) loves to sneak into my room, and I always have to check that she's not in there before I get changed. One minute we'll be arguing, and the next minute we'll be playing noughts and crosses while listening to a podcast. If you have siblings, you know what I'm talking about. Karma (one) also loves sneaking into my room, except she has an obsession with the wood chips in my plant pot. She'll sit there eating them for ages! I honestly can't believe I'm going to have a brother soon. My siblings are going to be like the three musketeers, except with less sword fighting and more trying to play with my makeup. Siblings steal your things, want to do everything you do, tell on you and even worse. Yet they can also be your best friend at the same time!

Tips for younger siblings (I asked Sienna for help with these.):

1. Listen to what they say and take their advice.
2. Don't tease them and stop if they say stop.
3. Respect them and their personal space.

Tips for older siblings:

1. Be the bigger person and don't let the little things get in the way of your relationship. I know that it's way easier said than done!
2. Your younger sibling may feel like they're in control, but remember back to when you were their age. Try to imagine how you would've felt and give advice, but remember that they may not always want it.
3. Be understanding. They're going to want to do all the things you do because they look up to you. Try to view the situation from their perspective and don't be too annoyed when they try to hang out with your friends.

Interview with SUPER SIENNA

Mia: Are you ready, Sienna?

Yep!

Mia: The first questions I'm going to ask you are about sisterhood.

Okay?

Mia: You ready?

Yeah!

Mia: Ready, Eddy?

Yes!!!! *laughing*

Mia: Okay, first of all: What is the best part about having sisters?

Umm . . . I would say that you've always got a friend to play with, even if they're not around the same age as you. If you've got an older one, then they can help you with different things like homework, or something like that. If they're younger then they're just like . . .

Mia: All cute?

Cute, yeah.

Mia: Dos: What's the worst part?

That sometimes they can be very, very annoying!

Both laugh

And sometimes they can, this is not really with you, it's more with Karma, steal your stuff!

Mia: Do you ever experience middle child syndrome? Or does it not affect you?

Ummm, no, not really. I'm fine with it. I mean, sometimes it is a bit annoying when I'm playing with Karma and then you want to play with her too.

Mia: Sorry about that.

It's okay.

Mia: She's just so cute!

I know!!!

Mia: What's been your favourite memory being a little sister? I.e., your fave memory with me.

It would probably be . . . I can remember that in America we were in your bedroom having loads of fun playing board games together.

Mia: Yeah, I remember that. Who won the most?

Me.

Mia: I can't deny that. Anyways, what's been your favourite memory being a big sister?

My favourite memory, for definite, was when Karma was born. I know it's probably your favourite memory as well.

Mia: Yeah!

It was just the sweetest moment ever.

Mia: I know, right! Okay, now it's time for some fun random questions.

Eeeee!!!!

Mia: Who is the messiest person you know? I feel like I kind of know what you're going to say about this.

You!

Mia: I knew it would be!

Both laugh

Mia: Seven: What is the worst smelling place you've ever been?

The toilet after . . . *laughs* After mum has been! *explodes with so much laughter it's incomprehensible what she's saying*

Mia: Sienna! Careful what you say! I don't think mum's going to like that!

Yeahhh . . . *still laughing*

Mia: Okay . . . If you had to change your name, what would it be?

Okay, wow. This is difficult! I've got quite a lot of names that I'd like, but one of my faves is Diamond.

Mia: Cool! I like that. Moving on, where's the one place you'd like to go most?

Oh, can it be like in the world?

Mia: It can be anywhere. Like a particular town, a particular street, a country or anywhere you want.

Space! The moon or Mars, just space in general.

Mia: I thought you'd say that. Now, the last and final question. It is very vital that you get it right. If I was a food, what would I be?

Uuhhh . . . if you were a food?

Mia: Yeah!

I'd probably say a . . . banana.

Mia: Banana? Why a banana?

Just because you remind me of one.

Mia: I remind you of a banana!!!

It's because you've got blonde hair and yellowish makeup, so it makes you look like a banana. I mean, that's the only fruit you could be.

Mia: *sarcastically* Well, thank you, Sienna.

laughs Sorry!

Mia: Anyways, thanks for letting me interview you, Sienna!

You're welcome. It was fun! Actually, one last thing, can I include something in your book?

Mia: Yeah, what is it?

This:

Mia: Awe, thanks Sienna! It's so sweet.

It's my best drawing and I tried really hard to make it neat. I drew me and my bunny, Cinnamon. I hope you like it!

Puberty

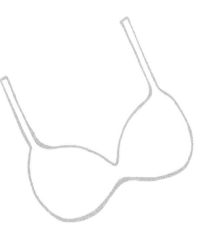

"It takes courage to grow up and become who you really are."

When I first started puberty it was really weird. When I was eleven, I went through a stage of having really embarrassingly bad body odour. I remember my auntie used to call me "Onion Girl" because I smelt so bad. Thank goodness I've gotten over that! Puberty can be really annoying, but it's nature and an important part of growing up, so you have to learn how to deal with it.

Not only have you noticed that you're growing boobs, but also now you need an over-the-shoulder boulder holder. There are many different colours, patterns, styles, and functionalities for bras. Make sure not to get too carried away, as you need to think about what types of tops you'll be able to wear with your bras. Then, you also need to find one that fits you! Definitely go get fitted. Lots of shops even do it for free. You may be nervous the first time, but it actually isn't that bad! I personally love sports bras, as they're super comfy, but I also wear a lot of strapless ones, as they work with lots of different tops. I recommend you experiment to see what works best for you!

♡ Don't sleep in your bra, as this can actually be bad for you! If you really want to, try a non-padded sports bra.

♡ Did you know your cup size varies based on your band size? A 32C is actually the same cup size as a 34B. These are called *sister sizes*, and if you're buying from a different brand than usual, you may need to get a sister size, as different brands have slightly different sizing.

♡ Store your bras with both cups open. Never invert one cup into the other because it destroys the fibres in the moulding, makes the cups bumpy, and it makes your bra not last as long.

Your first period can be quite scary. It's a completely new experience. Not only is it viewed as taboo, which I don't agree with, but also lots of girls aren't that educated about it. Luckily my mum was very supportive, so I had a nice first-time experience, and when I started I knew what it was immediately. I know it can be a bit scary and embarrassing to tell someone, but it's important to tell an adult female relative so you don't have to go through it on your own. They know what it feels like and have been through it. I've had my period for two years now, and it's definitely gotten easier as time's gone by, but it's still not a trip to the beach!

♡ Sanitary protection – There are tampons, disposable pads, reusable pads, menstrual cups and more! I recommend looking up all the options and experimenting to find what's best for you. I use either disposable pads or tampons during the day depending on what I'm doing. Then at night I like to use reusable pads.

♡ Emotions – I find that I can get very emotional when it's my period. I feel like crying and laughing at the same time. If you haven't experienced this before, it is very strange. I'll also snap very easily without realising, so it's important to try to notice when you feel funny, and remember that it's just because of your hormones.

♡ Timing – Mine always comes at the most annoying times. I'll either be on holiday and want to go into the pool, or it'll be a celebration where I just want to feel good. My tip is to ALWAYS be prepared. I always like to bring some sanitary products with me because even if you don't need them, you might be a lifesaver to one of your gals. I normally have a little purse which I pack with tampons and pads, but you can put any essentials you might need in there.

♡ F O O D ! Chocolate, ice cream, pizza and best of all . . . doughnuts, preferably deep-fried. When it's your period, be prepared for cravings. I recommend not fighting them, but instead, making an agreement. NO to Ben and Jerry's, but maybe yes to Halo Top? Have lots of dark chocolate on hand, as not only is it full of magnesium, which helps relieve cramps, but also it satisfies those sweet cravings. Eating lots of fruits and vegetables, avoiding coffee, and going for a light jog really do help you feel better, even when all you want to do is crawl under the covers for the next year.

Acne can be part of being a teenager. It always comes at the worst times, but you just have to deal with it. I haven't found a way to completely cure my acne, but I do find some things help. Drinking enough water, eating healthily, and getting enough sleep always help me. Some people find cutting out dairy or oil can also help. If you wear makeup, make sure to check the ingredients. It can help if you get more natural and even oil-free products. You also need to make sure you're removing your makeup properly and generally avoiding putting harsh chemicals on your skin. I like to use the white towel test because you'll be surprised, even when you can't see an ounce of makeup left on your face, there still might be some. After washing and drying your face, get a dry white towel and rub it gently on your skin. Is it completely clean, or is there a bit of product left on the towel? If there is, you need to get scrubbing! (Not literally, be thorough but gentle!)

Body hair can be really weird and embarrassing. You suddenly relate to when people say, *"If you eat your crust, you'll get hairs on your chest!"* more than you ever would've liked. Whether you decide to remove it or not is totally up to you. My mum decided to remove her leg hair when she was ten because it was really dark. I didn't remove my armpit hair until I was twelve, and I still don't regularly do my legs because my hairs are pretty much the same colour as my skin. I normally use a razor, because I feel like that's the least painful, and it's super quick for me to do my armpits. I have also tried waxing my legs, but it didn't really work because I got bad-quality strips.

♡ Shaving – Easy and quick, although depending on your hair growth you do need to shave regularly and you can get ingrown hairs.

♡ Depilatory creams – This is cream that dissolves the hairs. You don't need a prescription, but be careful because not all are the same. Always check that you're using it in the correct place and that you're not leaving it on for too long, because this can cause burning.

♡ Waxing – I made a video where I tried an at-home kit for the first time, but you can also get it done professionally. This can be messy and painful and might still leave hairs behind because they break off.

♡ Laser hair removal – This is one of the longest-lasting methods, but normally requires four or more treatments four to six weeks apart. The laser beam or a light pulse will destroy the hair bulb. This treatment can be expensive and painful, but it's used on many parts of the body.

♡ Electrolysis – is done professionally by placing a tiny needle with an electric current into the hair follicle. It is also currently the only FDA-approved permanent hair removal method.

Sometimes I can be a real SILLY BILLY. I'm super clumsy and I get confused easily. Lots of my friends say this happens to them as well, and it's apparently because of hormones. I can do such awkward things, like knocking over products in the supermarket and falling over, and my mum always asks me to do the laundry, but I get so muddled on what she wants me to do. It can help if you make sure you're eating enough, drinking enough water (the brain's 80 percent water, after all) and try to focus on one thing at a time, but there's not really a specific fix.

And that is just the tip of the iceberg! If you want more info, I've made lots of YouTube videos on my channel about this, but don't feel nervous to ask an adult or older sibling questions.

Squad

"Anything is possible
when you have the
right people there to
support you."

I was starting year five and I was quite upset because we had to swap around classes and I did not end up with the people I wanted to. I'd made loads of friends in my old class, and even though we'd be next door to each other, I knew it just wouldn't be the same anymore. So since I didn't have any close friends in my new class, I ended up talking to a girl I'd only ever said a few words to before. It was strange because even though she lived a few houses down from mine, I'd never thought of us being friends because we had totally different friendship groups. But once we started talking, we couldn't stop! We soon became inseparable and would spend all of break time with each other. But then my family said we were going to move. I was excited to go to a new place, but it would mean having to say goodbye to my new BFF, and it was a bit sad. I remember that a few days before we moved we even had a special goodbye sleepover, and we had loads of fun staying up and talking about random things. A while after moving into the new house I sent her a letter, and it took her a while to reply, but when she did, she included half of a friendship necklace. Then when I answered back to her, she never sent me another letter!

Like that example, I've found my best friendships haven't come as I expected. You may be surprised, but sometimes the perfect friend is right in front of you, but you don't even realise it. This doesn't mean sit at home all day and wait for fate to give you friends, but be open and proactive. Have you tried talking to the girl that sits in front of you in class? Or the boy across the road? You may never know what you're missing out on. There are loads of ways to make friends, but here are a few to get you started:

- ♡ Join clubs, as the people there have similar interests as you, so it's a great way to start off the conversation.

- ♡ Joining a fandom is a great way to make IBFs. Of course, be careful with this because there ARE weirdos out there. But as long as you're on guard, I know this can be an amazing way to use the internet.

- ♡ Talk to people! I know, I know, talking to people you don't know can be a bit scary, but it's important to remember that everyone's human.

Even celebrities! They have hopes and dreams, and most importantly, they want friends just as much as you. Rather than going on your phone while you're on a bus, start up a conversation with the person next to you. And if you do make a complete idiot of yourself, well, hope you never have to see them again!

Maintaining friends is just as important as making them, but sometimes you do have to leave people behind. Whether you move or grow apart, it happens and is a part of life. It can be difficult, but as time goes on, sorry to say, but frankly, you will get over it. Sometimes you may lose a friend because you've both changed, and this will happen at some point in your life. If you became friends five years ago, your interests and how you behave should have changed. This can happen together or it can end up that you don't get along anymore. You can try to talk to your friend, especially if you've been friends for a long time, and ask them how they feel. However, sometimes you have to accept that you're going to have to move on. I've had friends move house, and I've moved away from friends as well. You can try to keep in contact, and I still talk with some friends I've moved away from, but at the same time, there are a lot of people that I don't talk to anymore. At first, it will feel sad not to be friends anymore, but maintaining a long-distance friendship is very difficult, especially if you don't go back to where you moved from. Sometimes it's best to focus on the now rather than spending a lot of your time trying to make a past friendship work.

Most people have experienced bullying at some point in their lives, whether they were the bully, being bullied or just on the sidelines. It's scarily common, and we need to stop this. Nobody deserves it. Don't listen to the haters, as often they are projecting how they feel on you. Some people will always be negative, and there's nothing you can do about it, but don't let them affect your happiness. Here are my best tips to avoid the hate:

♡ **Don't keep it to yourself.** Always inform a responsible adult if you're experiencing bullying. No one should have to deal with this by themselves, and keeping it bottled up can actually be really unhealthy.

♡ **Radiate self-confidence.** If you're being bullied, it doesn't mean there's anything wrong with you. In fact, there's something wrong with the bully. Unfortunately, you can't change other people, but it won't do any harm to try to become your best self. Put on a brave face by standing tall and keeping your chin up, and that will convey the message: "Don't mess with me".

♡ **Get your mates to back you up.** Having a friend with you will give you more confidence when facing a bully, and the bully is less likely to give you trouble if they see there is more than one of you. This can also be a two-way exchange! Always get involved if you see bullying happening, by telling an adult, sticking up for the person being bullied, and telling the bully to stop.

♡ **Block.** If you experience hate online, my best tip is to block the hater and move on with your life. That person is clearly stuck in a rut, and rather than pulling themselves out, they try to pull others down to their level. They put you down because they feel bad about how they're doing in life. Wasting your time on them is exactly what they want, so don't give them that satisfaction!

Sometimes people feel like their friends have to be perfect, but some of the best friendships are between people who are different. I find that my best friends come when I'm least expecting it. Remember to not get too caught up on finding friends and appreciate the people you already have in your life; then the friend will come.

Your Personal Space

And remember,
nobody's life is more
complicated than
your own... Make time
to love yourself!

Although spending time with family and friends is great, I find if I spend too much time with other people, I go just a lil' cray cray.

Finding your own space can be surprisingly difficult. I love my bedroom because it's like an escape from the rest of the hustle and bustle of the house. You wouldn't believe how much noise two little sisters can make! But I know lots of people have to share rooms (more on that later), so you might have to get your space elsewhere. Maybe it's a quiet spot in your garden or at your local library, or maybe you could ask your parents if you can use the cupboard under the stairs as a den. You could buy a small rug, bean bag, and some fairy lights to make it super cute and cosy.

Of course, once you've found your space, you need to keep it nice. Since mine's my own bedroom, when I keep it nice, I feel like I sleep better and get on with more work! My room has white walls and wooden furniture with yellow and green decorations. I feel like the white makes the room feel clean and also makes the other colours pop more, and the wood makes you feel like you're in nature. I love to have bright colours because they make me feel motivated and look really aesthetically pleasing.

♡ **Let air come in.** Every morning I open up my window and let my room air out. This always makes me feel better because I'm not breathing in stale air. If possible, I'll leave my window open all the time, but of course, sometimes it's too hot/cold to do this, so just having it open for half an hour in the morning is still better than nothing.

♡ **Keep it tidy.** I know, I know, state the obvious, but this is actually something I need to work on. I have a tendency just to put something to the side and say, "I'll put it away later", which of course never happens. I do this so much that by the end of the day it's a complete tip! I have to train myself to do things immediately. If I don't it's never going to happen.

♥ **Organize your drawers.** It can be difficult to keep things tidy if you don't have any drawers or organisers. Whenever I have a specific place to put something, I'm more likely to put it there, so this hack is a must for me.

♥ **Make your bed.** Kind of following on from keeping things clean and tidy, if I don't make my bed, it makes my room look way messier than it actually is! This is one thing I pretty much always do straight away in the morning, but if there's ever a day where I'm in a big rush and don't get round to doing it, it always starts the day off on a bad note. When you make your bed in the morning it tells your brain that you're going to be productive and you get a sense of satisfaction for completing a goal so early.

♥ **Use essential oils.** You guys can probably tell that I like good air. I love having an oil diffuser in my room because it really sets the energy. At night, I love lavender because it really relaxes me, but in the morning I like something more energetic to get me pumped, like mint.

I've shared a bedroom with Sienna before, and there are definitely ups and downs. I think the most important thing is to make sure you get time apart. If not you'll end up arguing all the time. If you can't have a whole room to yourself, have a section that's yours. Agree with your sibling on an area that's theirs and one that's yours. Trust each other not to go fiddle with that, and leave each other's things alone. If you have bunk beds, this is great because you can keep some special things on your bed and tell your sibling not to go on it. Or have a rota and try to use the room when they're busy. I know it's difficult to have your own space when you don't actually have any, but focus on the benefits: there's someone in the room with you when you sleep, which can feel really comforting, and you always have a shoulder to cry on! The grass on the other side always looks greener, but it doesn't mean that it actually is, so make the most of your situation.

Once you've found some physical space, you also need to have mental space. What I mean by mental space is time where you're not doing anything and you're free simply to think. My ideas always come when I'm trying to sleep, as that's when my mind has no distractions. The only thing about this is that you lose out on sleep and the ideas you come up with might not always make a lot of sense since you're tired, lol. Try to set aside a small amount of time during the day (it can literally be two minutes) for doing nothing. Just sit down and stare at the ceiling. This gives your brain time to breathe. Of course, there are other (even more productive and less boring) ways of doing this. For example, you can exercise without listening to music or anything else. Whether you go for a swim or run, it doesn't matter, just as long as your brain has space to do its thing. This is a win-win since it's good for your mental and physical health.

Travelling

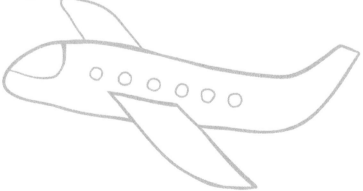

"If your child's adventure

is dangerous in

remote, it's lethal."

*I*t was my twelfth birthday and I was in Steve-nage, UK. I went to the cinema, and my parents got me a new laptop, but the best present of all was happening the very next day. We were moving to another country! We'd been to Gran Canaria multiple times before, sometimes even for a whole month, but this time it was official. I was ecstatic! When we arrived at our destination and moved into our apartment, it felt so good. I'd imagined moving abroad for so long, and it was amazing to FINALLY be doing it. After a while, I decided that I even wanted to go to school there (I was being homeschooled before). I started a school where they spoke Spanish, English, German and Mandarin! I could only speak English and very basic Spanish, so I was really nervous that there was going to be a huge language barrier. Luckily, my classmates had been learning English since they were very little, so they were fluent! I still had to take some classes in other languages, which was a bit difficult, but the teachers gave me some extra help. After about six months my parents told me we were going to move back to the UK because we had more opportunities there. I was a bit sad to be leaving, but I was excited about a new chapter.

You guys always ask me why we travel so much and if I feel sad about it. One time someone even asked what we're running away from! Well, I'm going to spill the beans, once and for all. Why I travel so much:

I love it!

My first time ever going on a plane was when I was eight. (If you want to be technical, I did go on one when I was a baby, but I don't really count it.) It was an eleven-hour flight to Sri Lanka! I slept for most of it, but the airline did give me a T-shirt as a souvenir. It was way too big for me, so I used it as a nightie for years. I wasn't scared of flying, and I'm still not, but it was weird to think that I was in the middle of the sky. When I arrived, even the airport looked different from the one in England! It was all sand coloured, and I even saw some ginormous ants. But that was just the beginning because when we got a taxi to the place where we were staying, I remember being really culture shocked. The sun was so hot, and there were palm trees everywhere; some even had coconuts and bananas!

We stayed in Sri Lanka for a whole month, travelling around the island. We visited the super-busy cities, went on a LOT of tuk-tuk rides, drank loads of fresh coconuts (they were only about twelve pence each), and even stayed in the jungle. It was so magical! One time, we were staying at the beach, so we decided to go down to a cafe that was on the seashore nearby. I was drinking a really nice mango smoothie when suddenly we noticed that some of the staff were throwing ping-pong balls at a monkey that was in the trees above us. I think they were trying to scare the monkey away, but it didn't work. In fact, they just angered the monkey, and it was SO scary because it had massive teeth, but I did feel sorry for it. It jumped down onto a branch next to our table and bared its teeth. We quickly ran away, but because Sienna was a toddler, she didn't know that it could hurt, so she stayed put! Eventually it went, but it was so terrifying. The whole time tourists kept taking pictures and the staff kept on throwing balls, which just made it angrier!

Another time while we were in the jungle, I was sitting on my bed relaxing and talking to Mum, when she said: "There's a snake behind you". Of course, I thought she was joking, so I laughed and turned around. To my horror, sure enough, there was a snake on the wall about forty centimetres behind me. I quickly ran away, and I was absolutely terrified. The snake was only small, but we had seen some really big snakes outside, so it was petrifying to think they had a way into our cabin. We called the staff, and at first they didn't understand what we were saying. They had no idea how it got there! They set the snake free, but that whole night I couldn't look at the wall because I was so scared! I'm not especially scared of snakes, but the thought of one slithering on me while I slept was horrible!

I think my favourite part about travelling is seeing new things. I love that feeling when you don't know what you're going to look at. This has only happened a few times (normally when I'm super tired), but it's amazing to wake up and not know where you are. I know this isn't everybody's cup of tea, but I'm a Sagittarius, after all. Travelling makes me happy! I feel my best when I'm somewhere I've never been before. My travelling goal is to go to all seven continents. So far I've been to Europe, Asia and North America. I feel like the most challenging one is going to be Antarctica, but that will probably make it the most memorable.

I understand that a lot of people don't have the time/money/means to fly to other countries, but that is only one way to travel. In fact, when I was little, my parents used to collect coupons from newspapers so we could go on weekend caravan trips. One time we went camping in Wales, and it was so scenic. You could stay at another family members house one night, or have a sleepover at your friend's house. Take a different route to school or the shop to see new things. There's also this site called Skyscanner, which shows you the best, cheapest and fastest flights available. I just checked, and for a family of four to get tickets from London to Barcelona it costs about fifty-five pounds. It obviously depends on the time of year, but you'd be surprised, cheaper tickets do exist. Or you could ask your school to go on a trip. If you get some friends to join you and tell them how educational and beneficial it could be, they may agree!

1. **Be prepared.** Have an audio/e-book downloaded or even a movie if the plane doesn't already have TVs. Don't forget earphones and your charger! ALWAYS, ALWAYS, ALWAYS wear comfy clothes (I have learnt from past experience), and I love letting my skin breathe by not wearing makeup.

2. **Get cosy.** You might as well take advantage of all this sitting down with nothing to do with a bit of self-care. Cuddle up with a blanket and put on a face mask! You need to keep your skin hydrated.

3. **Guzzle lots of water.** On the topic of hydration, to have an enjoyable experience you need to drink a lot of water! I know, you may end up annoying the cabin crew by asking for a drink every thirty minutes, but with all that recycled air it's really important. (Bonus tip: try to drink loads while the seat belt sign is off so you can use the bathroom.)

4. **Take your shoes off.** When you're in the same position for a long time it can be really bad for your circulation. If you take off your shoes it helps with that, and it's super comfy.

5. **Take vitamin C.** The worst thing is when you arrive at your destination, ready to have loads of fun, and then you get a bug. Airports and airplanes, let alone the new country, have loads of new germs that your body isn't used to. Try to eat lots of fruits of vegetables and take vitamin C lozenges to help build up your immune system. An apple a day keeps the doctor away!

6. **Learn about the place you're going!** Have some guidebooks on hand, or download articles onto your phone. If you want to learn a bit of the native tongue, there are loads of language-learning apps you can download, such as Memrise

A re you ready to do something that you've always thought was impossible? Get ready to time travel with me . . .

. . . to 2011 when I was six years old. This was taken on a trip to see my grandparents, and I remember that this jumpsuit was my favourite thing to wear. I'd always save it for super special days. Don't forget to apply suncream!

We're still on course in 2011. This pic was taken
when Mum was pregnant with Sienna.

Now you can see her bump! And our cat, Elmo.
She used to hate kids so much, I think I only
managed to stroke her about five times, lol.

We would go on walks past this field full of ponies, and I always used to stop to feed them grass! Look at him nibbling away.

And finally, Sienskies is here! She's so cute.

I'm out on a walk in the woods, and of course, my best
friend Jofli came. I took him everywhere with me.

For my seventh birthday I had a bee-themed
party! We all dressed up, even little Sienna.

*Going for another walk. Don't worry about Jofli.
This time I remembered to wrap him up.*

Sienna's first Christmas!

It's still Christmas 2011. I just felt like modelling this tinsel headband. (Spy the homemade snowflakes in the background: that is something I'd do every year).

This pushchair was meant for a baby doll, but why play with a toy when you have the real deal? I loved pushing Sienna around in this, as you can see by my smile.

2013, in the woods with Mum.

I'm not entirely sure what I was trying to make for Jofli here, but let's just say it's his warrior costume. (I have no idea why there are teeth on the headband, but moving on).

Ready for a birthday party, dressed in my bunny costume. Can you see my missing rabbit teeth?

Me on my eleventh birthday in Gran Canaria!

I don't stop sipping . . . do I?

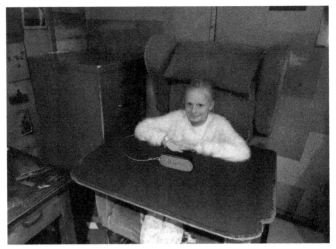

*At the Roald Dahl museum in London. This is a replica
of the chair he used to write his books from!*

*The YouTube studio in London with Sienna.
Look at her fringe . . . awweee!*

Me and Sienna tried making an ice cream sundae . . . without ice cream. (Yes, that is mash potato.)

Pancake Day 2017

*Throwback to when I dyed my hair
unicorn colours. It looks so cool!*

Sienna did my makeup . . .

When little Karma was born.

She's so cute!

Christmas 2018 in Copenhagen, Denmark.

Welcome to Las Vegas, baby!

When my mum and Darren got married at the Grand Canyon!

Money

"Money equals

freedom."

I t was 8:00 a.m., and I was buzzing. Ten-year-old Mia had just come up with an AMAZING idea. I quickly told my parents about it, and I got to work. I always have this thing where I'll be trying to sleep and then out of nowhere I get an idea, and if I don't get it down on paper immediately, I'll lose it. So with the words swarming around my head, threatening to escape, I wrote a story. If I remember correctly it was about a hamster who wanted to be free from his cage. Once I'd written it, I designed all the pictures in the e-book myself, then hired somebody to format the book, and lastly I put it onto a self-publishing website. Unfortunately, the book didn't end up getting any sales, but I had so much fun working on it that I actually started another one.

Just because you're not an adult yet, it doesn't mean you can't start making money. As kids, my mum got paid to do the ironing for her nanny, and my stepdad, Darren, bought cheap sweets and then sold them to his friends at school. Now is one of the best times to start a business because you don't have all the liabilities adults have. Even if you don't make much, it's so fun to spend and save your own money for the first time. Make sure to ask a parent about this first though. They may even give you some advice.

♡ Make physical projects and sell them on Etsy (like slime).

♡ Ask family or a neighbour to pay you for doing housework, babysitting or doing another job which you know you can do well.

♡ Buy bargain products from charity shops and resell them on eBay.

♡ Create a YouTube channel and make money from ads. This one does require a lot of effort, though, as you're not allowed to monetise until you have at least ten thousand subscribers.

♡ Swagbucks is a site where you can get paid for just using the internet! The points you earn are put into a "bank" and can be redeemed for gift cards to be used on Amazon or at local and online stores.

♡ Have a clear-out and sell things you don't need/ want but could be valuable to someone else online or at a car boot sale.

♡ Collect cans or water bottles and give them to the recycling centre. Check out what the area where you live accepts, and you can even ask your neighbours if you can collect their rubbish. This is good for the planet too!

If you do decide to start making money, make sure you enjoy it and have fun with it. If you want, you can even team up with a friend! There are so many opportunities; you just have to keep an open mind and be ready to act when they arise.

Once you've actually made money, believe it or not, it can actually be pretty difficult to manage. There are a lot of things you can do with money, like saving, investing in an asset (something you gain money from) or spending it on a liability (something you lose money from). It's up to you. Before you start using it, though, I recommend that you do a bit of research. There's an author called Robert Kiyosaki, and he has a book called *Rich Dad, Poor Dad*. He also has an edition for teens, video games, a comic and more, all designed to help you learn about money. You should definitely go check them out!

Another thing you can and should do with your money is give. I know it can feel a bit scary, but if you're not willing to donate £1 when you have £10, you're unlikely to give £1,000 when you have £10,000. Saving is important, but you can't hoard. Besides, money loses value because of inflation, so you might as well use it while it's worth something. Of course, if you can't give financially, you can give your time or expertise. You could make cakes for a charity sale or volunteer at an animal sanctuary.

You may think buying the cheaper option is the best choice financially, right? Well, that's not always the case. I always used to buy really cheap flip-flops, and of course, you get what you pay for. They were really bad quality and would break almost immediately. So I decided to save up a bit and invest in a more expensive and better-quality pair, and I've had them for six months now and they're as good as new, so I know they're definitely going to last. If I haven't already, in the long run I'm going to save money by buying the better pair. I'd have to buy a new £15 pair every three months, so it would take a year for me to even out my spending on a better-quality £60 pair. I made sure that the flip-flops could go with a lot of things. I love them because I can use them for casual flip-flops to the beach, but because they have a sparkly bow and look quite fancy, I can also wear them as smart sandals. This approach is also better for the environment because you're creating less waste. However, another way to shop is in charity shops. I've found some really cool pieces in there, and if you like getting crafty, you could make some clothes more your style! Another amazing tip is that in some shops, like H&M, they have this recycling bank where you can take your old clothes and they'll give you money-off vouchers in return.

If you really want to learn about money, I recommend that you ask your parents for a bank card. You could even ask to join in with the process of going to the bank and filling in the forms. My parents have a card for me where they can put in money, and I know that lots of my friends have this. It's super handy because if you don't have any cash on hand, your parents can easily transfer a bit of pocket money onto the card.

At the end of the day, money is a really important part of life. Money doesn't make you happy, but it gives you the freedom to do what you want. Using money as a tool is a skill that school doesn't teach, but it is one of the most valuable life lessons. Having a good relationship with money and knowing how to use it is really important. Get out there and start learning!

Fashion

Beaty

and

Hair

'Style is a way to say
who you are without
having to speak.'

When I was little I used to have a very ... to put it nicely ... strange fashion sense. I can remember wearing what I thought back then was fashionable, but was actually really embarrassing. One time when I was eleven I got denim dungarees that I thought looked really nice. Don't get me wrong, I do like dungarees, but they definitely do not suit me! I look like a minion in them.

I don't tend to have a particular style. One day I'll wear something floral and girly, but the next day I'll wear something sporty. That's what I love about fashion: you get to decide who you're going to be that day. One of my favourite videos to film on my channel is when I completely change my style, like when I dressed as a goth for twenty-four hours. Even though it was just what I looked like, it made me feel like a whole new person!

But it can take a while to work out what you like to wear. What are your go-to pieces? Mine are jeans, a cropped tee, and trainers. What is your favourite item in your wardrobe? What do you never wear? Go through your wardrobe and give the things you don't need to charity shops or donation centres, then write a list of any essentials you might need. Research outfits on Instagram or 21 Buttons, and find things that suit you and you feel confident in, not just things that are on trend.

Striped flared leggings and pink top. I love this outfit because I feel like it has boho vibes and is so comfy!

Jeans, purple mesh top and black crop top. This
outfit is super cute because you can go crazy with the
accessories! I really love this pearl clip and holographic
bag, but you could switch it up with a backpack or
headband, depending on what you're feeling.

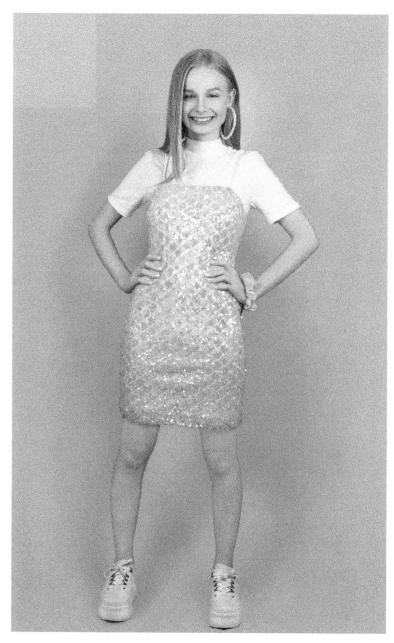

Sparkly pink dress, white tee and sparkly earrings. This dress is so fun because you could dress it up with some kitten heels, or dress it down with a tee and trainers like I have. Also, I love how the dress and earrings match!

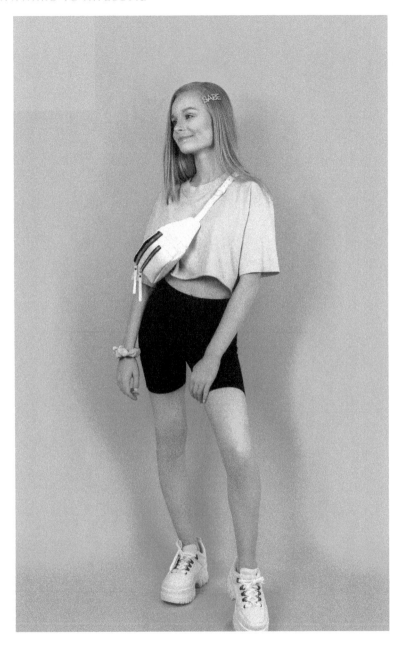

Blue crop top, biker shorts, babe clip and
bumbag. My favourite type of clothing is sports
clothes. They look super trendy, make you feel
like moving and are sooooo comfortable.

I'm petite, so I find it really difficult to find clothes that are for my age and actually fit! Most shops just have women's clothing (which is too big for me, even in the petite section) or kids clothing (which can be super babyish, as the clothes for fourteen-year-olds are just bigger versions of the ones for seven-year-olds). Though there are some shops which I've found are good for tweens/teens:

♡ **New Look 915 Generation** – This is my fave shop EVER!

♡ **Brandy Melville** – The clothes are all women's size 4–8, so some things are too big for me, but they're super cute!

♡ **River Island** – They don't have a teen section, but I find that the kid's clothes aren't too baby-ish here. I have tried on the women's, but they do NOT fit! Size 6 is ginormous on me.

- ♡ Lululemon – The tees don't fit me, but the cropped leggings are the BEST! I love athleisure because it's so comfy and makes you feel like getting active.

- ♡ Topshop Petite – Again, not everything fits, but I've found some good things.

Accessories make or break an outfit. Sometimes I love wearing colourful earrings and headbands or gold hoops with a scrunchie—it all depends on my mood and outfit. Sunglasses are super practical, but look amazing if you get the right pair. My favourite type is the more classic styles, but I always see people wear these really thin cat-eye glasses, which I'd love to wear, but I don't think they really suit me. I have four piercings (one lobe in both ears, one tragus and also my nose), but I'd love to get some more. I think helix piercings look really nice, and I also love upper lobe piercings, but I think I'd have to go to a place where they curate your ears in case it looked like too much.

It took me a lot of experimentation to find makeup that was right for me. I'm a redhead, so a lot of colours won't suit me, and I'm also prone to acne, so I try to find stuff that isn't too bad for my skin. The worst struggle is doing my eyebrows because they're so light you can't even see them! A combo that has been working for me lately is using the Tarte Busy Gal BROWS tinted brow gel in Taupe and the Urban Decay Brow Box in the shade Blondie. For a long while, I also found it really difficult to find eyeshadow that didn't make me look like I'd been punched. I'd always use muddy brown, and it looked terrible! But I've been using orangey brown lately, and it actually looks good, so it's made me feel a lot more confident and adventurous when I do my makeup. I also love to do a bright-coloured eyeliner, as I think it makes your look more unique and draws attention to your eyes.

♡   Tarte   I love this brand because they use natural ingredients and their makeup is oil-free.

- ♡ **Urban Decay**   I especially love the Hi-Fi shine lip glosses because they are the longest-lasting lip gloss I've ever used, and they have loads of colours.

- ♡ **Kat Von D** ♡ The eyeliners DO NOT budge even if you rub your eyes.

- ♡ **ELF** ♡ I love this brand because they're affordable and really good quality. I especially like the primers.

- ♡ **Too Faced**   All of the products look and smell so good! I love the sweet peach collection because the lip glosses even TASTE like peaches (not that I recommend eating them, lol)!

= Not all products have 100 percent vegan ingredients, but they are NOT tested on animals.
♡ = 100 percent vegan ingredients and NOT tested on animals.

I always buy makeup that is 100 percent vegan and isn't tested on animals because it's horrible and unnecessary that animals have to go through pain just for us to look pretty! There are loads of brands that aren't tested on animals, and just as many vegan products that work as well as non-vegan products. Being vegan is all about doing your best and avoiding harm to animals, so I don't eat animals or anything that comes from them; wear leather, wool or silk; or use cosmetics that have been tested on animals or have ingredients derived from them. I also don't visit zoos or aquariums, as I don't see why animals should have to be imprisoned just for our entertainment, especially when you can go to a rescue centre or visit them in the wild! I've been vegan since I was eight, and it's something I'm never going to go back on.

On my channel, I love trying out beauty treatments for the first time. I once tried getting my eyebrows tinted, and it was amazing! Because it was my first time, the lady at the salon did it quite light, but it lasted a few weeks. I definitely think it was worth it, but I wish it lasted a bit longer. You can get at-home kits, but I'd be too scared in case they went wrong.

I've also tried fake tanning, which was quite weird for me because I'm naturally super pale. I think it's good if you want to look tan without the sun damage, but I definitely wouldn't do it all the time because it's very messy and takes up a lot of time. If I went to a special event and wanted to look tan, I think I would do it again because I get burnt easily and sun damage is really bad for you. When I tried an at-home kit, it didn't last that long, but it did make a difference. But when I got it done professionally it was way stronger and lasted longer. At first I was a bit nervous because you obviously can't wear any clothes, but in the end, I realised that it's the lady's job so she has to see it all the time.

I love doing things with my hair, especially braiding and curling it, but halfway into doing the hairstyle I get incredibly bored and frustrated. My hair is reasonably thick, so I find it difficult to get it to obey me! I also find it annoying how they'll always have blonde hair bands for thin and medium hair, but for thick, only black! If I do use the others they stretch, snap and won't even hold my hair in place. I like to wash my hair every two to three days, but sometimes I leave it longer and let it get really greasy. I find this really helps my hair stay in good condition, and it's a huge time saver because washing my hair takes ages. My best hair tip is something that I only learnt recently: double shampooing. It will transform your hair game! I feel like the first time doesn't really lather that much, but on the second go, you look like you're in a shampoo ad.

Step 1: Part your hair in the middle from forehead to nape and separate two small pieces of hair at the front. (These won't be part of your buns.)

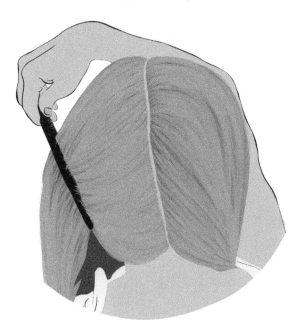

Step 2: Put the two big sections into tight high pony-tails. The tighter the better!

Step 3: Twist hair away from your face.

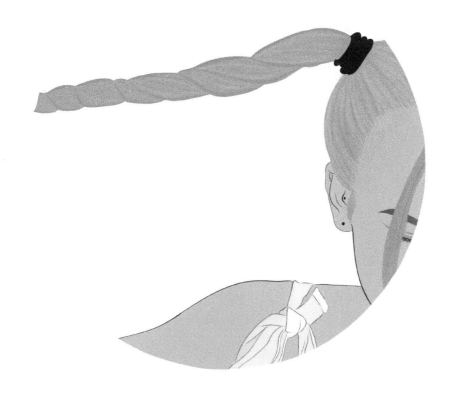

Step 4: Spiral your hair into buns and secure with clear elastics and bobby pins.

Step 5: Done!

Step 1: Part your hair in the middle, leaving two small sections at the front.

Step 2: Grab a medium-sized section of hair and tie up into a ponytail with a clear elastic.

Step 3: Repeat on the other side and you're done!

Step 1: Part your hair all the way down the middle, and tie up one section.

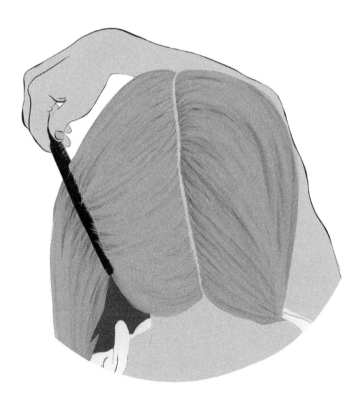

Step 2: Start Dutch braiding by splitting a small section of hair into three.

Step 3: Bring the left section underneath the middle section so it's the new middle section. Repeat this one more time, except take the right section to the middle this time.

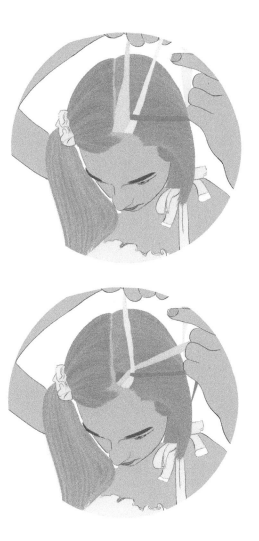

Step 4: Carry on doing this until you reach your nape, except every time you bring a piece to the middle, grab more hair.

Step 5: Tie the braid with a clear elastic. If you want you can wrap around a section of your hair to cover the hair band and use a bobby pin to secure it.

Step 6: Untie the first section and repeat the last four steps.

Step 7: Now pull on your braid to make it bigger and use a bobby pin to fix any flyaways. Additionally, you can curl your hair that's not in the braid for a fancier look!

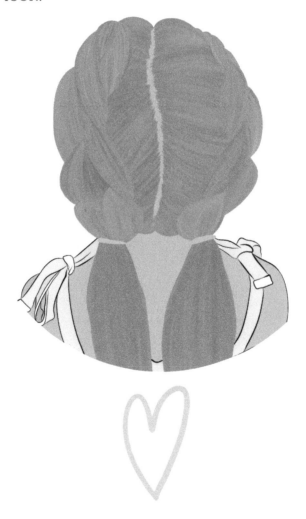

Going Out by Yourself

"The most courageous
act is still to think for
yourself. Aloud."

The first time I went out by myself I was nine and it was to my school. I obviously knew the route very well because it was only about ten minutes away and I'd walked it hundreds of times, but to be extra sure, my mum walked me halfway there and then let me do the rest by myself. After that trial run, I walked there more or less every day by myself.

When we moved to London, I had to get the bus to school with my friends. I found it so crazy getting to experience the manic morning and afternoon commute every day! It was like the whole population came out at the same time. Businessmen and women in smart suits, people opening up stores for the day and commuters arriving from outside the city to start their jobs.

While going out by yourself can be super fun, you do need to be careful. As long as you're sensible and stick to the rules, going out by yourself is part of becoming an adult and can really change your perspective on the world. I was definitely a bit nervous at first, but it's important to get used to not relying on your parents all the time.

1. Always have your phone with you and double-check that it's charged! You may need to call someone or use a maps app if you get lost.
2. Tell your parents what your plans are and keep them up to date if they change.
3. Stay alert and pay attention to your surroundings!
4. If you're out while it's dark, stay in well-lit public places, preferably with a group of friends.
5. Even if a road's quiet, always check before you cross.

You might not be the only nervous person. At first, your parents will be too! It's important to remember that this isn't just a big step for you; it's also a big deal for them to let you out into the world. What makes this more difficult is there isn't really a perfect age for them to let you go! It's all dependent on where you live and how mature you are. If you live in the countryside, you might be allowed to go to the local park when you're eight, but if you live in the city you might not be allowed out until you're thirteen.

♡ **Get them to trust you by doing rather than saying.** You can do this by respecting what they say, doing what you say you're going to do, and getting your chores out of the way before they even ask you to! It's kind of common sense: if you're constantly breaking the rules in the house, what are you going to do out of the house? They'll never trust you! However, your parents aren't stupid. If you suddenly spend all morning offering to give your mum a massage and doing the washing up and then ask them, they'll know what you're doing. This is a gradual process that takes time.

♡ **If they're worried about your safety, get a friend they know is responsible to come with you.** This will give them peace of mind, and if your friend's having the same problem, it might help them out too!

♡ **Listen and try to understand their concerns.** The reason they worry is because they care about you.

♡ **Talk about possible solutions.** Your parents might want an older sibling to come with you. Even if you don't want this, remember that if your parents are willing to let you go, you have to be willing to accept some of their conditions.

Food

"There is no sincere love
than the love of food"

Soo . . . you've probably noticed that I've mentioned food just a tad. Well, a lot. If you couldn't already tell, I'm definitely a foodie. But quite often I like the strange foods that everybody else thinks are weird. When I was little, every time someone asked me what I wanted to eat, you'd think I would've said fast food, ice cream or sweets. But, no. All I wanted to eat was sushi! I also hated any spice, so much so that I thought sweet red peppers were spicy. I have no idea why because they're called SWEET peppers for a reason. As I've gotten older I've actually started liking spice, especially wasabi (I'm still obsessed with sushi).

I think what's really made me appreciate food is being vegan and also travelling. When you go vegan you end up trying loads of new foods. Sure, you might not like everything, but you'll also discover something that you would've never tried that you actually love! The same goes with travelling. I love to try different countries' food because I feel like you really get to experience the culture that way. My favourite cuisines are Japanese (I just can't stop talking about sushi, can I?), Mexican (You can't beat quesadillas!!!!), Italian (Who doesn't love pizza?), Brazilian (Açai is the best! And it's also full of loads of antioxidants)—the list is endless. Honestly, every time someone asks me that question, my answer changes depending on what I've just eaten.

However, I'm not the best chef. I can make some good things, but my cooking skills are not amazing. But I have found some recipes that are easy enough for me to make that are super delicious (and are also really quick)! Trust me; if I'm capable, you are!

Umm ... who isn't obsessed with avo on toast? I love to make this for lunch because not only is avocado full of loads of healthy fats which is great for your skin, hair and nails, but also it tastes amazing!

You will need:

- 1 ripe avocado
- two pieces of bread (My fave is sourdough, the thicker the crust, the better.)
- 1 lime

Directions:

1. Put your bread in the toaster for about 1-2 minutes, depending on how you like it.
2. Cut your avocado in half. Then place one half on each slice.
3. Mash your avocado using a fork. Then squeeze on some lime juice. You can also add in some pepper, or if you don't have lime, use lemon!

This food section wouldn't be complete without my fave food . . . donuts! I love these because they're baked instead of being fried, which means there's less oil and they're way easier to make. Also, this recipe makes twelve mini donuts, so there are plenty to share! (Or, if you really want, you can just hog them all yourself, lol.) And, as if they could get any better, these only take twenty minutes of food prep, then ten minutes of baking time!

You will need:

- ♡ 1 cup white flour
- ♡ 1/2 cup sugar
- ♡ 2 teaspoons baking powder
- ♡ pinch of salt
- ♡ 1/2 cup soya milk
- ♡ 1 teaspoon vanilla extract
- ♡ 3 tablespoons apple sauce (I couldn't find any apple sauce, so I had to use puréed apple baby food instead, lol.)
- ♡ 1/4 cup coconut oil
- ♡ tinfoil

Directions:

1. Preheat your oven to 180°C (355°F).
2. Combine all the dry ingredients in a large bowl and stir thoroughly.
3. Add in all the wet ingredients and mix until it's a doughy texture.

4. Pour the batter evenly into a greased muffin tray. I find that when I put a small amount of batter, they look more like donuts and less like muffins.

5. Get twelve 2-inch-wide strips of tin foil and roll them up so they're quite thick. Poke these into your donut so they have a hole.

6. Bake them for 8–10 minutes. You'll know they're cooked if you can poke them with a toothpick and it comes out clean.

7. Once they're done, leave to cool for about 15 minutes, and then remove the tinfoil. Now it's decoration time! If you're feeling lazy you could just add some sprinkles, or alternatively, you could top them with melted chocolate, multi-coloured icing, fruit and sweets.

Okay, this might officially be the simplest recipe in the world (if you can even call it a recipe), but not a lot of people know about this amazing combo. This is the perfect snack and only takes about two minutes, max!

You will need:

- 1 apple
- peanut butter

Directions:

Slice your apple up and get a spoonful of peanut butter for your dip. Yep. That's it! I also love adding a bit of cinnamon, or if you want something sweeter, try adding some syrup to the mix!

Smoothies are great because you can basically put anything into the blender and you're done. Here are some of my fave combos:

- ♡ **Chocolate and PB** – Cocoa powder, chocolate soya milk and peanut butter.

♡ **Berry blast** – Any of your fave frozen berries (mine are cherries and raspberries).

♡ **Piña colada** – Chunks of pineapple and shredded coconut.

Directions:

Chuck any of these combos into the blender and then add **2 ripe bananas** and some **soya milk** (unless you're making the Chocolate and PB Smoothie, since you've already got the chocolate milk). That's it!

There's definitely a theme going on here . . . These cookies are so quick and easy, but most importantly, delicious. This recipe makes 9 cookies.

You will need:

- 1/2 cup peanut butter, or if you're allergic, you could use another nut/seed butter, or (believe it or not) you can actually get peanut-free peanut butter. I bet that's something you thought you'd never hear.
- 3/4 teaspoon baking soda
- 3 tablespoons white flour
- 1/3 cup sugar
- handful of chocolate chips
- pinch of salt
- 2 tablespoons applesauce
- 1 teaspoon vanilla extract

Directions:

1. Preheat the oven to 180°C (355°F).
2. Combine the dry ingredients in a large bowl. If you can't mix your peanut butter, then gently warm it up until it softens.
3. Then add all the wet ingredients and mix until it's a doughy consistency.
4. Separate the batter into small balls, and then flatten them and place on baking paper on a light-coloured tray.

5. Bake for 6 minutes. They won't look done when they come out but will harden over ten minutes. DON'T remove from the tray before they've completely hardened. If you do, you'll just end up with a sticky mess.

Happiness

"Happiness is a choice, not a result. Nothing will make you happy until you choose to be happy."

You guys always ask me how I'm happy all the time. Well, the truth is, I'm not. I feel like people have this thing where they believe that if you feel any emotion other than happiness, it's a bad thing. This is so not true! If humans only felt happiness, we wouldn't even know we were happy or appreciate it. Trying to achieve the goal of being happy 100 percent of the time is not, well, achievable. What IS achievable is a "positive mindset" There is a difference. Okay, imagine this scenario:

You're on the start line for the 50-metre sprint. You've been training for this competition for a month. Every morning you've been getting up early to practise, and you're determined to come in first. The whistle blows and you're off. The world around you goes blurry, and all you can focus on is the sound of you running as fast as your legs can carry you. But just as you cross the finish line, you notice that some of your competition has already made it! It turns out that you came in eighth, in a competition of ten.

Now, if you were trying to be 100 percent happy, you'd start jumping up and down out of joy.

Yeah, 'cause you're going to start doing that.

However, if you had a positive mindset, you'd be thinking, "So, I didn't meet my goal, but I'm proud of myself for trying. I know my competition has been training for a longer time than me, so I'm going to do that next time."

As you can see, there's a big difference between the two. In one you don't even take in the fact that you didn't meet your goal, so you're never going to learn from it. In the other, you can learn from the experience. However, in neither are you angry or sad that you didn't make it. In general, there's nothing wrong with these emotions, and you shouldn't try to avoid them, but when you have a positive mindset you try to focus on the good rather than moping about all day. Because just like being happy 100 percent of the time, you don't learn or grow from that.

When you have a positive mindset, you try to accept your feelings. But you have to remember that sometimes feelings can be affected by inside things. I normally never would cry because my phone ran out of battery, but if I'm super overtired or it's my period, I might do, lol.

Your health controls a huge part of how you feel. If you're tired and fuelling your body with rubbish, of course you're not going to feel your best. I like to drink at least eight glasses of water a day, avoid eating rubbish throughout the week, and get ten hours of sleep. Of course, you're not going to be able to do this every day, but having balance is important. On weekdays I like to be really healthy by eating lots of greens, going to bed early and going to the gym, and on the weekends I like to have my treats. This feels great because I have some structure and I know that while I do love eating healthily, I'm still going to have some not-so-healthy things without feeling bad, because I'm supposed to be eating them.

Being mindful and grateful can change your life. The quality of your life is whatever you decide it to be, and if you actually step back and notice all the positives, you will realise that life is amazing. There are many ways to practise mindfulness. You can go for a run or simply look out the window and take in the fact that you're alive, here and now. I know that being mindful can seem complicated and you don't know how to start, but it's that thinking that stops you. Being mindful is paying attention in the present moment nonjudgmentally. Practise mindfulness in the mundane everyday tasks like brushing your teeth. Be aware of how the toothpaste smells and how the bristles feel.

Helping others is actually a great way to help yourself! Not only will you be putting out positive vibes, but also you'll have good things to work on. Some easy ways to help out are by spending time with a grandparent, cleaning the beach with some friends or creating a social media account where you write good things about people.

Only consuming positivity is a major way to notice more good. If you're constantly watching bad things happen on the news, consuming negativity on social media and spending time with people who constantly moan, you're unlikely to notice the positives. You're not going to be able to remove all negative sources, but if you try to combat them by making a vision board, following positive social media accounts and being with friends that uplift you, it can make a huge difference on your outlook in life.

Having goals and something to work towards is such a powerful thing. Not only will you get the satisfaction of feeling fulfilled, but also you won't have time to notice negativity. I've gone through phases where I feel down or unhappy, and I've found that it's when I have nothing to work towards. When I have goals and I'm doing things I feel hyped about it really brings up my energy. Start small, like making your bed every morning, rather than overwhelming yourself. One thing lots of people find useful for sticking to goals is to use your pride to your advantage. Whether you post it on Twitter or tell a friend, getting it out there that you're going to stick to a goal will force you to do so. You also need to make sure you're constantly being reminded of your goals. Having a vision board is a great way to do this, and it's loads of fun to make!

You will need: 1 pinboard, pins, magazines, and leaflets and/or printer

1. Write down all of your goals. Have big lifelong goals, like buying your dream house, and smaller ones which you can complete in a few weeks, like learning how to roller skate.
2. Find pictures related to your goals. If you want to eat healthier, get a picture of some vegetables. If you want more friends, get a picture of people having fun. You can cut out

things you find in magazines or print pictures from online.

3. Lay them all out on your vision board and get pinning!

4. Now you need to put your vision board somewhere you're going to see it. This can be on your wall, inside your wardrobe (so every time you get changed, you look at it) or on your bathroom mirror.

What I love about this concept is that you can adapt it to your needs. Don't have a pinboard? Just glue pictures to a piece of paper. This does mean you'll have to start from the beginning if you want to change it, but it does the job. I actually like to use a digital vision board. If you use a collage app, you can create an amazing vision board because you can choose whatever pictures you want, and it's better for the environment! Set the digital vision board as the background on your phone, tablet or computer, and you'll be surprised by how many times you see it. I pick up my phone about twenty-five to thirty times a day, so I see my goals a lot.

The internet is such an amazing invention, but have you ever gone down that rabbit hole where you spend hours on Instagram then wonder what on earth you've done? I've been there. There's this phrase:

OUT OF SIGHT OUT OF MIND

You can do this physically by leaving your phone at home, getting a friend to hide it or anything else that forces you to not use it. Or, if you're like me and actually need your phone, delete any time-wasting apps. I know you may be tempted to download them again, but just the act of not seeing them when you go on your phone really does help.

You guys always ask me for advice, so I thought it would be fun to do a little agony aunt section. I asked you guys to give me some of your questions on Instagram and loads of you replied, so I've tried to answer as many of you as possible!

When people say negative things about others, it's a reflection of how they feel. Think about a day when you felt amazing. Would you have gone out of your way to make others feel bad? No, in fact, you would have probably done the opposite! This girl is obviously unhappy and is trying to make herself feel better by making you feel bad. Don't let any of her words affect you, and stick with your friends. A true friend won't believe in gossip and will come to you to support you.

Consistency and authenticity are key. There are millions of channels, so think about what's going to make people want to follow YOU. Find a niche that you feel passionate about, but don't feel scared about evolving and growing over time.

There's always something "good" just as there is always something "bad". It just depends on your perception. It's all about noticing the good and learning from the bad. For example, you forget to set your alarm and wake up half an hour before school starts, and it takes twenty-five minutes to get there! To add to that, you are in such a rush that you stub your toe—twice! This is the point where you need to take a step back and realise that it's not the end of the world (just for your poor toe). Learn from this situation to always, always, ALWAYS check if you've set your alarm, and be grateful for the fact that your mum offered to help you by making your breakfast.

This can be a difficult and stressful experience for you, but if you want to stay friends with both, you need to let them know how you feel. Say that you're on both sides and avoid getting involved in their feud. If one friend complains about the other, never engage in this criticism, even if it's to make one of your friends feel better, as it will slap you in the face later down the line. If they ask you to pass on messages to each other, let them know that you're not comfortable with being a go-between and tell them that they should say it to each other directly. Be kind to both and let them know that they're important to you and you want them to settle any disagreement.

Educate yourself on the benefits, and try to explain to your mum why you want to do this. She may be nervous about you becoming unhealthy, so tell her about how healthy it can be as long as you have a balanced diet. If she thinks it might be inconvenient, show her all the options you have. Nowadays every-thing has a vegan alternative, even scrambled egg!

I know this is going to sound a bit weird, but prac-tice makes perfect. The more time you spend around people, the less nervous you'll become. I know at first it can be difficult, but remember that everyone is insecure and gets nervous. Try taking baby steps. Maybe get a friend to come with you and introduce yourself to new people. That way you'll feel like you have some support.

Do the hardest task first. You have the most will-power in the morning, so it makes sense to force yourself to do your least favourite thing then. Once you have the boring (but important) things out of the way, then do what you feel passionate about. And lastly, don't forget to reward yourself!

Be cautious, but remember that people can change. Depending on the severity of what he did to you consider giving him a second chance. Listen to your instincts and take it slow. It might help if you get an unbiased friend's point of view on the situation. If this was years ago, then maybe a second chance would be a good option, but if this was only last week then I'd stay away from him.

Messi

Messing

UP

I have not failed. I've
just found 10,000 ways
that won't work!

Even if you've read this whole book and tried to implement the things I've said, you're still going to mess up sometimes. It's part of growing up, whether you like it or not. I find it's best just to make a joke out of it rather than stressing. Here are some super-embarrassing things I've done:

♡ I was in Norway trying to jump over a stream in front of my crush. Unfortunately, I tried about six times, and every time I fell in and got soaked! To this day my family still teases me about it!

♡ I was in year five, and I accidentally called my teacher (who was a MAN!!!) Mum! Luckily it was just as we were leaving the classroom, so nobody heard, except for one boy, who kept laughing at me.

♡ I was in a shop recording a video when I accidentally knocked over a bottle of liquid soap and it went everywhere! I said sorry to the shop assistant, and luckily he said it was fine.

♡ I was at one of my old schools and there was a really old chair there that was a bit broken. Me, being stupid as usual, tried to sit down on that chair. Of course, I fell right through the seat and got stuck! Everyone laughed.

♡ At my school in Gran Canaria there was a basketball court in the playground. One day, I was standing near the hoop minding my own business, when suddenly a basketball came whizzing directly towards me. I wasn't paying attention, and there wasn't enough time to move, so it hit me directly on the nose. It was so painful! I think this experience is probably where my fear of balls came from.

♡ My parents let me do a video on Family Fizz where I got to control their lives for a day in Dubai. I was super excited, and it was really fun at first, but during the day I decided I wanted to do a water sport. We ended up doing this thing called flyboarding, which is like a board with two jets underneath that propel you upwards. My stepdad, Darren, went first, and it looked like so much fun. Then it was my go. The first few tries were, well, tries. Then I started to get a bit of motion, but what happens when you go up? You have to go down. And by down, I mean belly flopping into the salty sea. Not very pleasant. Because of this, I ended up really hating it, so I kept trying to go up without going too high, but this just made me fall in more! I remember the guy saying, "Five minutes left", and me thinking, "No, NO more minutes!!" I'm glad I tried out something new, but I'm definitely NOT doing that again.

♡ This next one is another to do with water. I was on holiday in Bali and we had a pool at our villa. Sienna and Darren kept doing dives into the pool, so I thought: "I'll try". Easy, right? Well, no. I tried about five times, and every time I got really scared and it was a failure belly flop. Later on that day, a boy I'd made friends with that lived next door joined us in the pool. Of course, Sienna quickly told him about how "amazing" I was at dives. So, unfortunately, I ended up having to demonstrate just to get her to shut up. Luckily he said he couldn't do dives either, but it was embarrassing.

♡ I was walking down the street in Georgia, talking about something (I can't remember what) that I was really into. I was so engrossed in talking that the rest happened in slow-mo. I was holding Sienna's hand, so two seconds too late, she tried to pull on me and said, "Mia!" But as she said that, I felt something slimy and smelly squidge under my shoe. I then skidded a full foot down the pavement, and literally stood there for about thirty seconds in shock. Mum and Darren had stopped walking by this point, and everyone was laughing their heads off. I turned around, and sure enough, there was the biggest dog poo I had ever seen with a foot-long skid mark of it all the way down the path! Mum also filmed all of it on Instagram stories, and a couple walking near us was staring in disgust at the pile of faeces and my shoe. Yuck!

Share your awkward moments on social media by using the hashtag #awkwardtoawesome, and you might get featured on my Instagram stories!

If you never make mistakes, you're not learning anything. I prefer to think of mistakes as steps. That way you won't have any negative associations to them. Every time you take a step, you get closer to your goals.

YOUR
TIME TO
SHINE

You can write in the
sand or on a watermelon
or whatever you want,
but the best thing to put
out of your hand or half
in your head and keep
on your arm and even
something like you did

I love journaling, and if you haven't ever tried it before you definitely should. I've decided to leave some space in this book (with prompter questions) so anytime you want to write down your thoughts and feelings, you know where to go! In case you get stuck, I've dotted around some of my own answers.

Mia's Answer: I'm always optimistic and try to look for the good in situations.

_____

_____

_____

_____

_____

_____

_____

_____

_____

_____

_____

_____

Mia's Answer: My legs for being strong.

_____

_____

_____

_____

_____

_____

_____

_____

_____

_____

_____

_____

_____

Mia's Answer: Bright!

1. _____

2. _____

3. _____

4. _____

5. _____

Mia's Answer: Unfair gender roles.

1. _____
2. _____
3. _____
4. _____
5. _____

1. _____
2. _____
3. _____

_____
_____
_____
_____
_____
_____
_____
_____
_____

I want _____ to know that:

_____

_____

_____

_____

_____

_____

_____

Mia's Answer: I value kindness and treating others how I would want to be treated.

_____

_____

_____

_____

_____

_____

_____

Mia's Answer: I'm a simple girl to please: Food!

_____

_____

_____

_____

_____

_____

_____

_____

_____

_____

_____

_____

_____

_____

_____

_____

_____

_____

_____

―――――――――――――――――

―――――――――――――――――

―――――――――――――――――

―――――――――――――――――

―――――――――――――――――

―――――――――――――――――

―――――――――――――――――

―――――――――――――――――

Mia's Answer: Antarctica! I want to sleep on the snow and gaze up at the stars, not to mention see some penguins. It sounds so beautiful.

―――――――――――――――――

―――――――――――――――――

―――――――――――――――――

―――――――――――――――――

―――――――――――――――――

―――――――――――――――――

―――――――――――――――――

_____

_____

_____

_____

_____

_____

_____

_____

_____

_____

Mia's Answer: *"One thing only I know, and that is that I know nothing."* - Socrates

1. _____

_____

_____

2. _____

_____

_____

3. _____

_____

_____

4. _____

   _____

   _____

5. _____

   _____

   _____

_____

_____

_____

_____

_____

_____

_____

_____

_____

_____

_____

_____

_____

_____

Mia's Answer: My family.

_____

_____

_____

_____

_____

_____

_____

_____

_____

_____

_____

Mia's Answer: Travel to all 7 continents!

1. _____

2. _____

3. _____

4. _____

5. _____

6. _____

7. _____

8. _____

9. _____

10. _____

11. _____

12. _____

13. _____

14. _____

15. _____

16. _____

17. _____

18. _____

19. _____

20. _____

21. _____

22. _____

23. _____

24. _____

25. _____

1. _____

2. _____

3. _____

4. _____

5. _____
6. _____
7. _____
8. _____
9. _____
10. _____
11. _____
12. _____
13. _____
14. _____
15. _____

1. _____
2. _____
3. _____
4. _____
5. _____
6. _____
7. _____
8. _____
9. _____
10. _____

January:

1. _____

_____

2. _____

_____

3. _____

_____

February:

1. _____

_____

2. _____

_____

3. _____

_____

March:

1. _____

_____

2. _____

_____

3. _____

April:

    1. _____

       _____

    2. _____

       _____

    3. _____

       _____

May:

    1. _____

       _____

    2. _____

       _____

    3. _____

       _____

June:

    1. _____

       _____

    2. _____

       _____

    3. _____

       _____

July:

1. _____

_____

2. _____

_____

3. _____

_____

August:

1. _____

_____

2. _____

_____

3. _____

_____

September:

1. _____

_____

2. _____

_____

3. _____

_____

October:

1. _____

   _____

2. _____

   _____

3. _____

   _____

November:

1. _____

   _____

2. _____

   _____

3. _____

   _____

December:

1. _____

   _____

2. _____

   _____

3. _____

   _____

This year:

1. _____

   _____

2. _____

   _____

3. _____

   _____

4. _____

   _____

5. _____

   _____

_____

_____

_____

_____

_____

_____

_____

_____

_____

Person: _____

About: _____

Person: _____

About: _____

Person: _____

About: _____

Person: _____

About: _____

Person: _____

About: _____

Person: _____

About: _____

Person: _____

About: _____

Mia's Answer: Mandarin.

1. _____
2. _____
3. _____
4. _____
5. _____
6. _____
7. _____
8. _____
9. _____
10. _____

I have the right to **Ask whatever questions I want.**

I have the right to _____

_____

I have the right to _____

_____

I have the right to _____

_____

I have the right to _____

_____

I can **Do anything I put my mind to.**

I can _____

_____

I can _____

_____

I can _____

_____

Mia's Answer: The amazing opportunities life has brought me.

1. _____
2. _____
3. _____
4. _____
5. _____
6. _____
7. _____
8. _____
9. _____
10. _____
11. _____
12. _____
13. _____

14. _____
15. _____
16. _____
17. _____
18. _____
19. _____
20. _____
21. _____
22. _____
23. _____
24. _____
25. _____

_____

From: _____

_____

From: _____

_____

From: _____

_____

From: _____

_____

From: _____

To: _____

To: _____

To: _____

To: _____

To: _____

Hi, _____

_____

_____

_____

_____

_____

_____

_____

_____

_____

_____

_____

_____

_____

_____

_____

_____

_____

_____

Love,

_____

Mia's Answer: This one! lol. Also, *Sophie's World* by Jostein Gaarder

Book: _____

Author: _____

Book: _____

Author: _____

Book: _____

Author: _____

Book: _____

Author: _____

Book: _____

Author: _____

Song: _____

Artist: _____

Song: _____

Artist: _____

Song: _____

Artist: _____

Song: _____

Artist: _____

Song: _____

Artist: _____

_____

_____

_____

_____

_____

_____

_____

_____

_____

_____

Mia's Answer: I walked into a door frame. (It actually hurt quite a bit lol.)

_____

_____

_____

_____

_____

_____

_____

Mia's Answer: I should of payed more attention to where I was going.

_____

_____

_____

_____

_____

_____

_____

_____
_____
_____
_____
_____
_____
_____
_____
_____
_____
_____
_____
_____
_____
_____
_____
_____
_____
_____
_____

Acknowledgements

Wow . . . if you made it this far I give you a pat on the back (btw if you haven't read the book yet but want to see the ending, shame on you). But luckily you're not going to find out whether Alice made it out of the rabbit hole, but rather a special thanks to everyone who helped me in the making of this book:

Thanks to my amazing proof reader, Grammargal.

Thanks, Nadia from Divine Nine, for the gorgeous cover and Instagram pictures. It was so much fun working with you!

Thanks so much to Danna Mathias for designing my cover and interior.

Thanks, Sienna, for being an avid listener, even when my manuscript was only five hundred words. You're the best big little sister ever. Love you to Mars and back!

Thanks, Karma, for always toddling into my room and making me smile! You're too cute, *bebecita*. *¡Te quiero!*

Thanks, Darren, for always being there for me. You're the best!

Thanks to Mum for supporting me. I love you more than you can imagine!

And last but not least, thank YOU, dear reader, for supporting me in this incredible journey. I can't believe it. I have my OWN BOOK!!!! If you had told me about my life right now 5 years ago, I would have laughed in your face. Or been mind blown. Literally. But actually not literally, just in the incorrect grammar sense.

I love all of you,